… The **FIXER'S** Guide to…

SCREWS

Written by **JOHN WOOD**

Illustrated by **AMY LI**

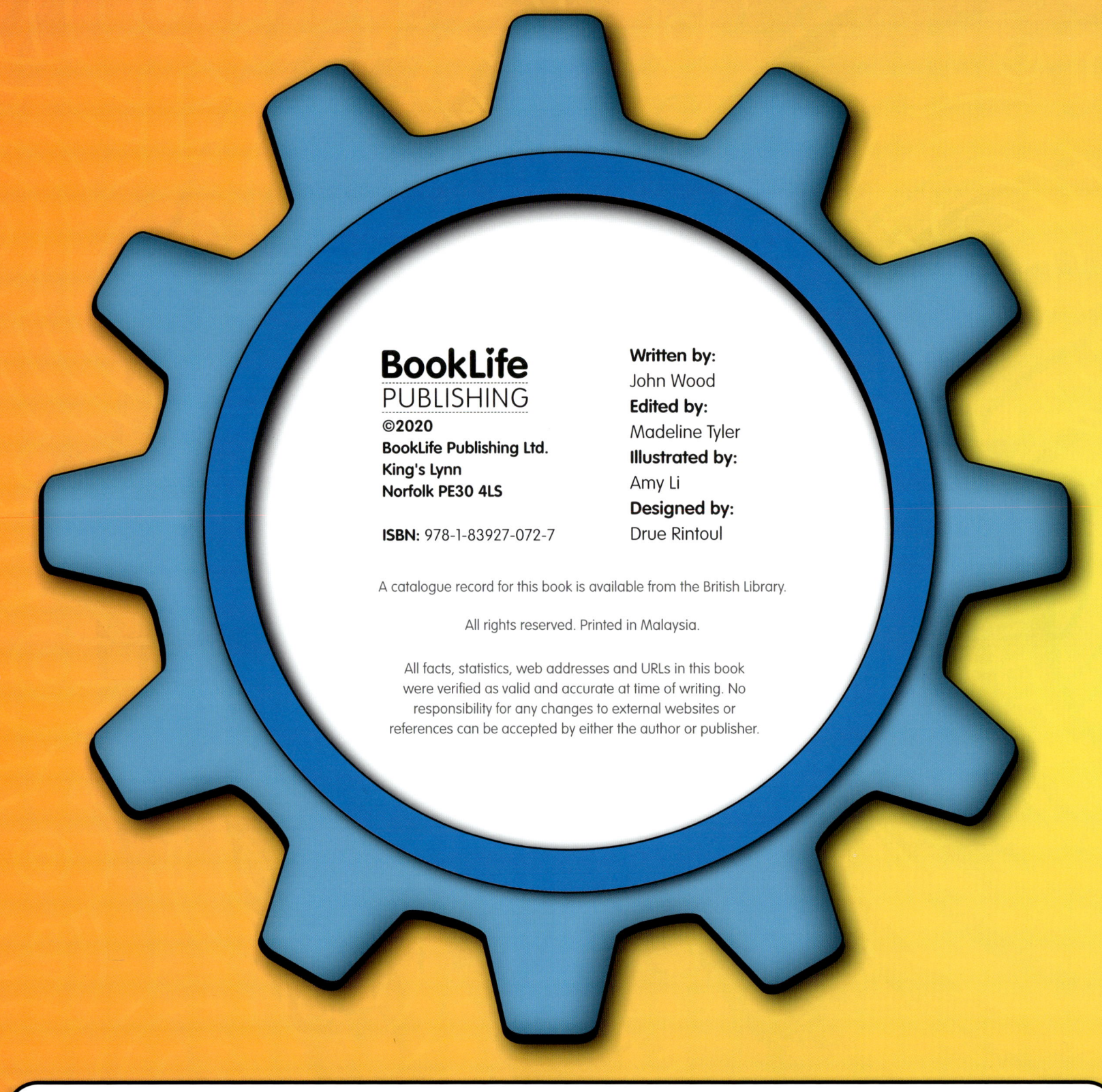

BookLife PUBLISHING

©2020
BookLife Publishing Ltd.
King's Lynn
Norfolk PE30 4LS

ISBN: 978-1-83927-072-7

Written by:
John Wood

Edited by:
Madeline Tyler

Illustrated by:
Amy Li

Designed by:
Drue Rintoul

A catalogue record for this book is available from the British Library.

All rights reserved. Printed in Malaysia.

All facts, statistics, web addresses and URLs in this book were verified as valid and accurate at time of writing. No responsibility for any changes to external websites or references can be accepted by either the author or publisher.

Photo Credits

All images courtesy of Shutterstock.com. With thanks to Getty Images, Thinkstock Photo and iStockphoto.

Recurring images (cover and internals) – Guliveris (background pattern), Agor2012, robuart (cogs), Steve Paint (arrows). 4–5 – volodimir bazyuk, Tartila. 6–7 – Natpant Prommanee, Panupong786, Nattasid Thapsang, OlegSam. 8–9 – Scisetti Alfio, Mrs_ya, Somchai Som, Mircea Moira, Naypong Studio, bofotolux, Binh Thanh Bui. 10–11 – Natan86, LittleElephant. 12–13 – LedyX, JIANG HONGYAN. 14–15 – Oleksandrum, FOTOGRIN, peart. 16–17 – Natan86, FabrikaSimf. 18–19 – Marnikus.

CONTENTS

PAGE 4	Meet the Fixer
PAGE 6	Screws
PAGE 10	Parts of a Screw
PAGE 12	Types of Screw
PAGE 14	How a Screw Works
PAGE 16	How to Make the Best Screw
PAGE 18	Let's Build a Spinning Top
PAGE 24	Glossary and Index

Words that look like this can be found in the glossary on page 24.

MEET THE FIXER

Look at this huge mess. This is the Fixer. He does this all the time. Say sorry, Fixer.

Pfflblululupgh.

Believe it or not, the Fixer is the smartest being in the universe when it comes to machines.

A machine is an object that makes a job easier to do. The Fixer wants to teach you about one of the simplest types of machine: a screw.

A wheelbarrow is a simple machine.

SCREWS

Screws are long and thin, with a <u>ridge</u> running around the outside. They are usually used to hold two things together. Although they look a lot like each other, screws are different to nails.

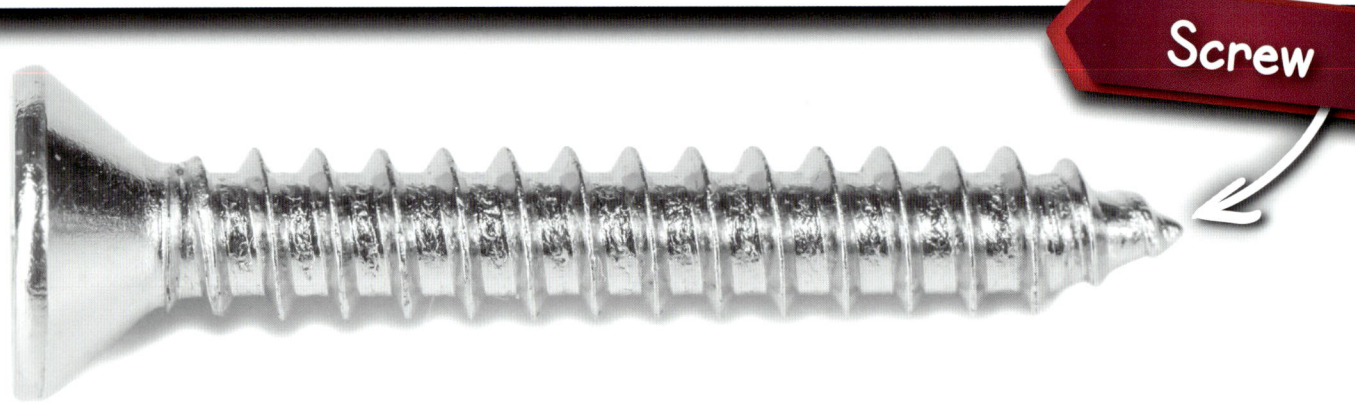
Screw

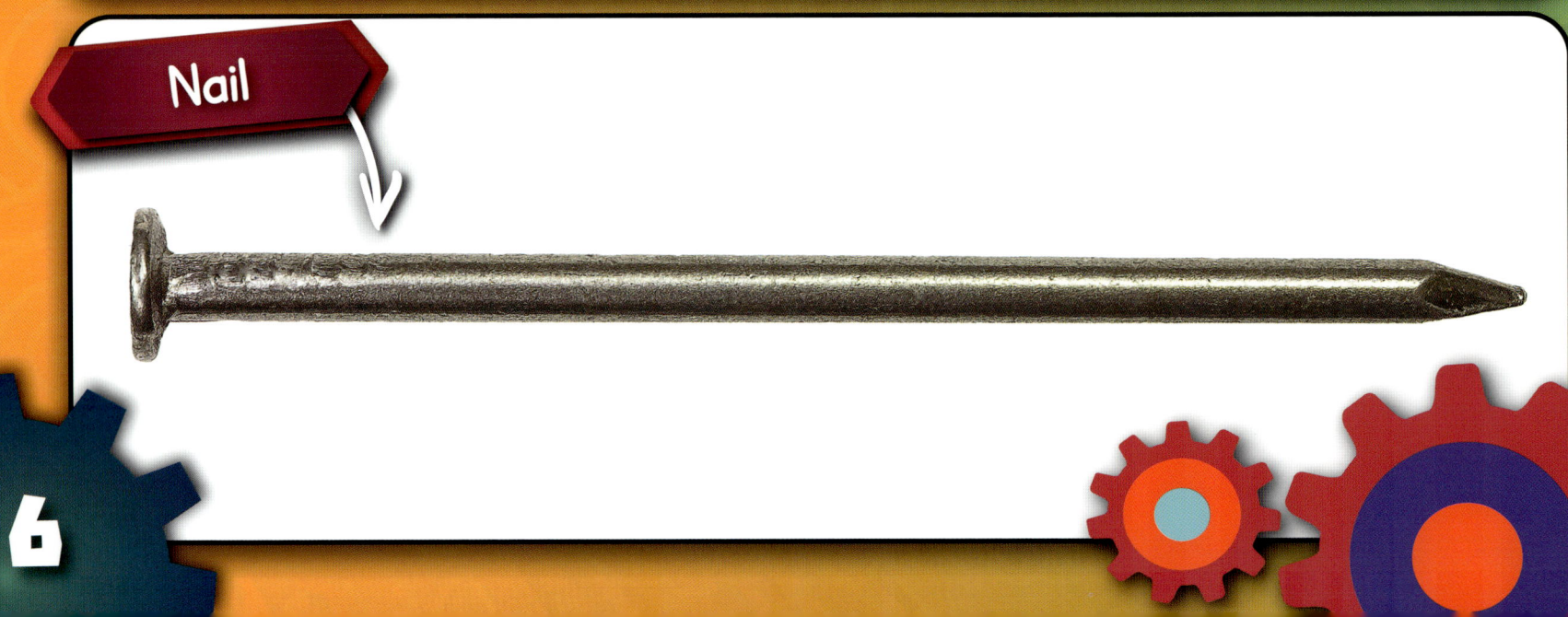
Nail

Nails do not have ridges, and they are hit into an object with a hammer. Screws need a twisting <u>motion</u> to force them into an object. A drill or screwdriver is used for screws.

Drill

Screwdriver

There are lots of different screws. Here are some screws that we see every day.

The lids of some pens are screwed on and off.

The tuning pegs of some musical instruments are screws.

Some light bulbs have a screw at the bottom so they can be fixed in place.

Plastic bottlecaps are a type of screw.

Cork openers

Some jar lids

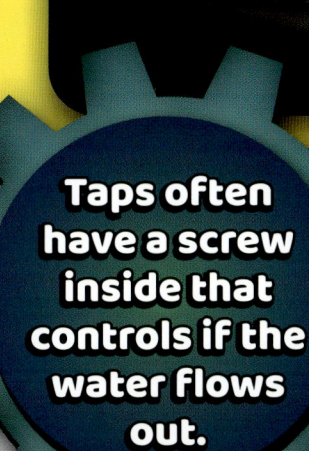

Taps often have a screw inside that controls if the water flows out.

9

PARTS OF A SCREW

There are four main parts of a screw: the head, the tip, the shaft and the ridges that run around the outside. The ridges are called the threads.

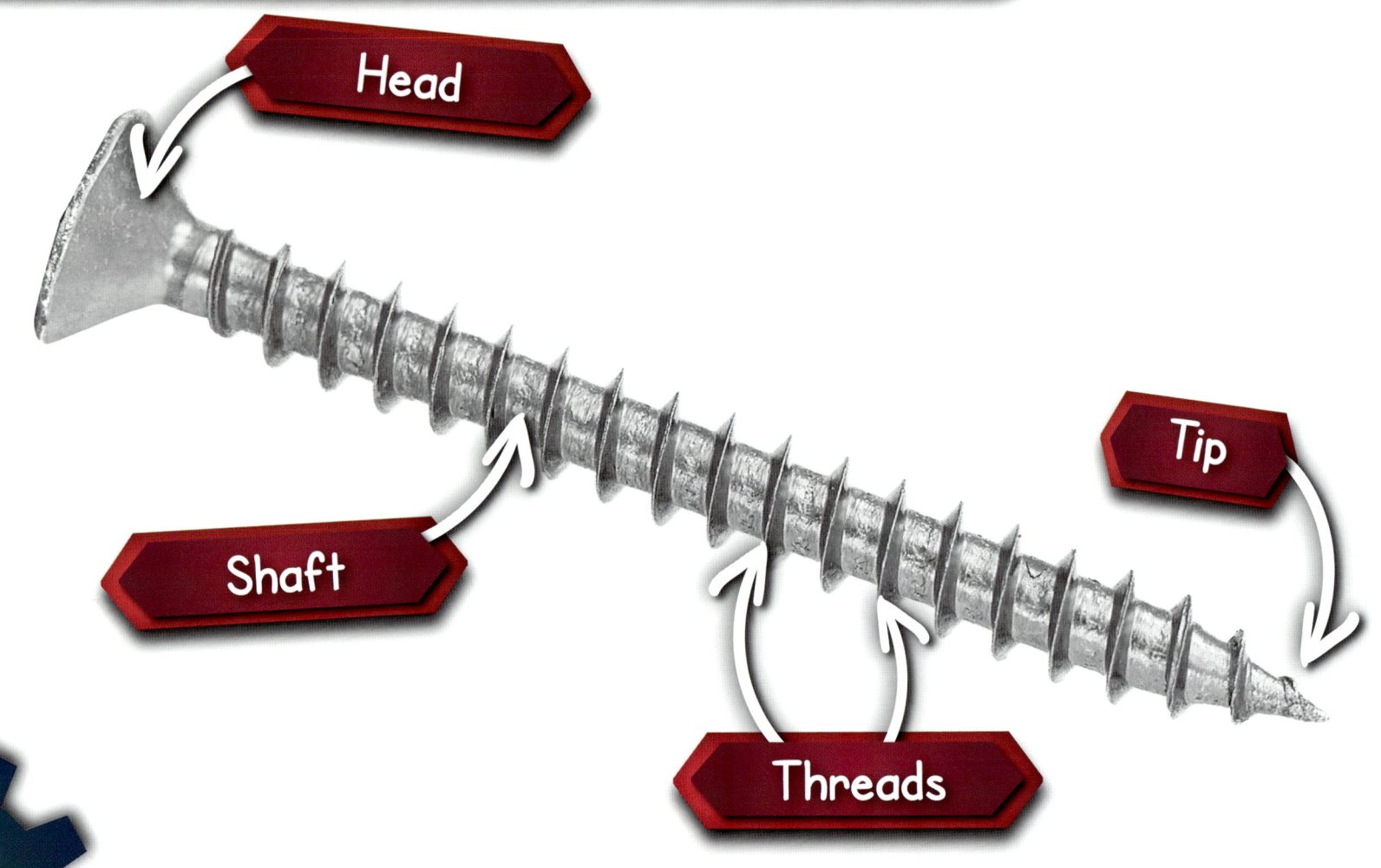

10

The tip is pointy and sharp. This helps the screw to go into another object. The head is wide and flat — this is the part that a screwdriver or drill fits into.

Screws like these are usually made out of metal.

TYPES OF SCREW

SSPHLUPLTLOO.

The Fixer is very excited. He says there are lots of different types of screw. He wants to show you a few with different heads. These screws need a screwdriver with the right end.

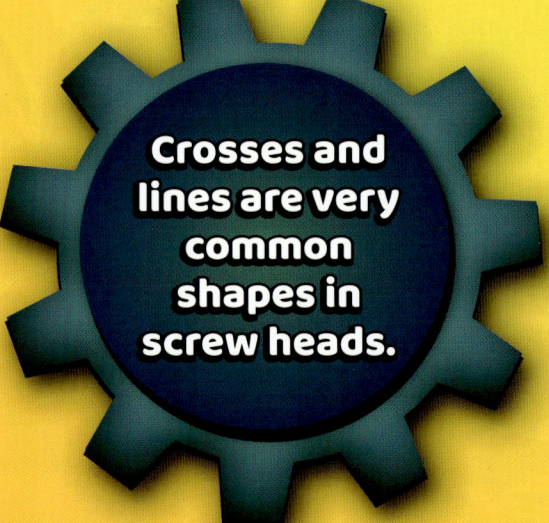

Crosses and lines are very common shapes in screw heads.

12

A bolt is like a thicker screw, and it comes with a nut. The nut is a piece of metal that screws onto the tip of the bolt after it has been driven through something.

The nut makes the bolt more secure.

Bolt

Nut

HOW A SCREW WORKS

A screw turns a twisting <u>force</u> into a downwards force. As the screw turns, it sinks into a <u>material</u>, such as wood or plastic.

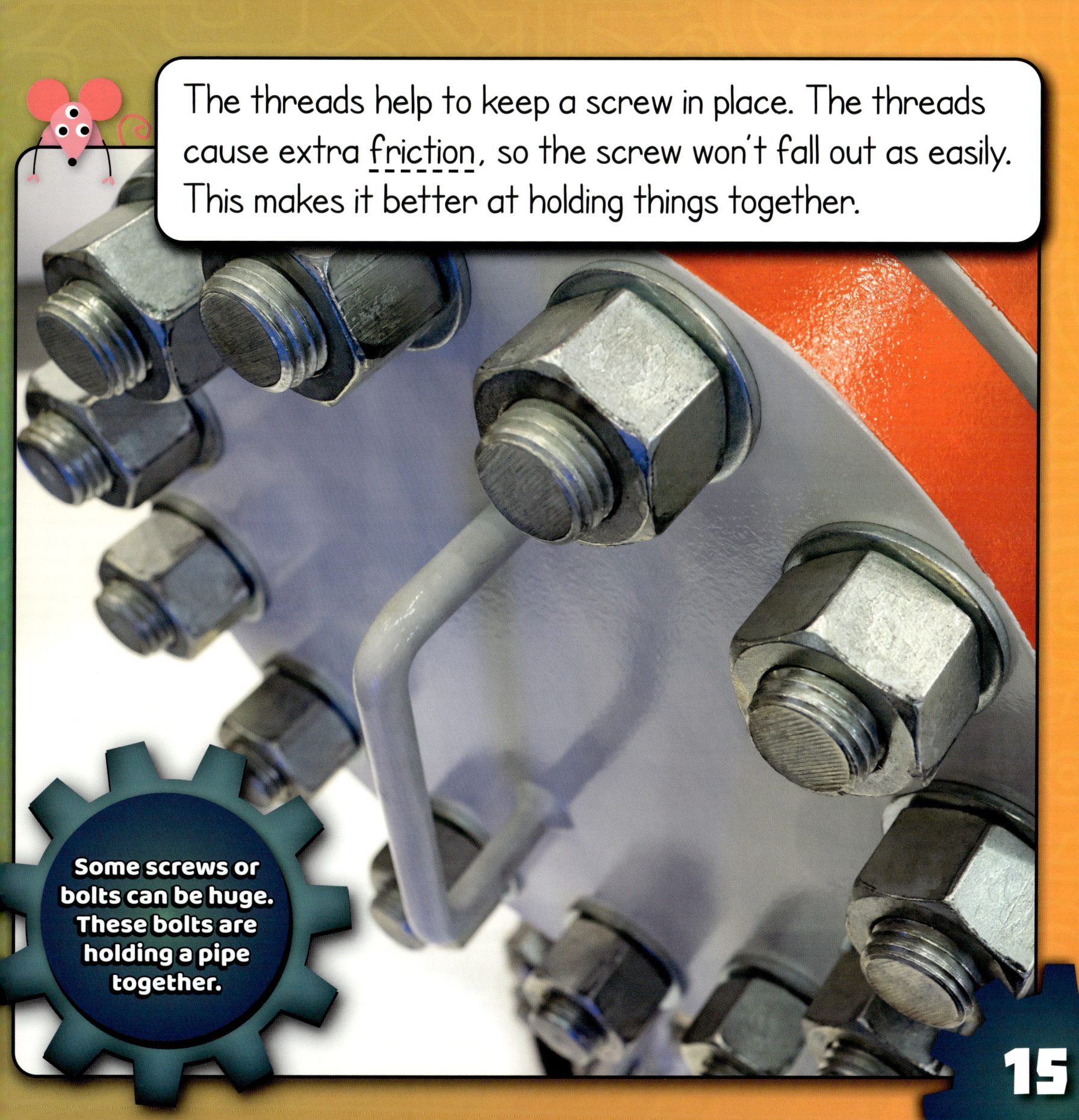

The threads help to keep a screw in place. The threads cause extra <u>friction</u>, so the screw won't fall out as easily. This makes it better at holding things together.

Some screws or bolts can be huge. These bolts are holding a pipe together.

HOW TO MAKE THE BEST SCREW

> PLKUSSSILDUMN.

The Fixer really wants to tell you what makes a good screw. He says it is mostly to do with how much space there is between the threads.

16

The less space there is between the threads, the less force is needed to screw it. However, it will take more turns. The more space, the more force is needed.

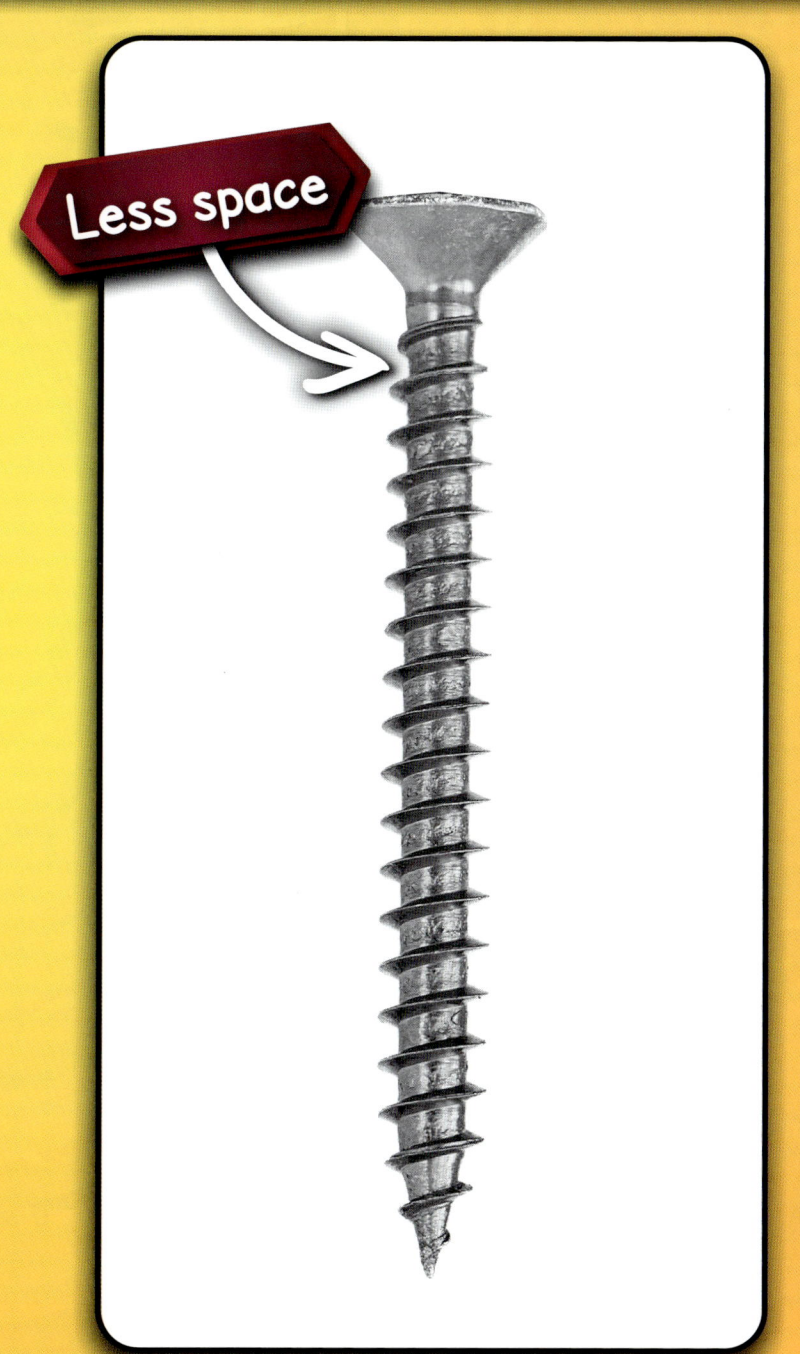

Less space

More space

LET'S BUILD A SPINNING TOP

It is time to build! We will be using a bolt to make a spinning top. Get an adult to help you with the drilling in step 1.

The toy will also use a magnet.

YOU WILL NEED:

- A long, thin bolt
- 2 nuts that fit the bolt
- 2 light wooden discs
- A small magnet that will fit on the bolt's head

Extra materials: Bendy metal wire

19

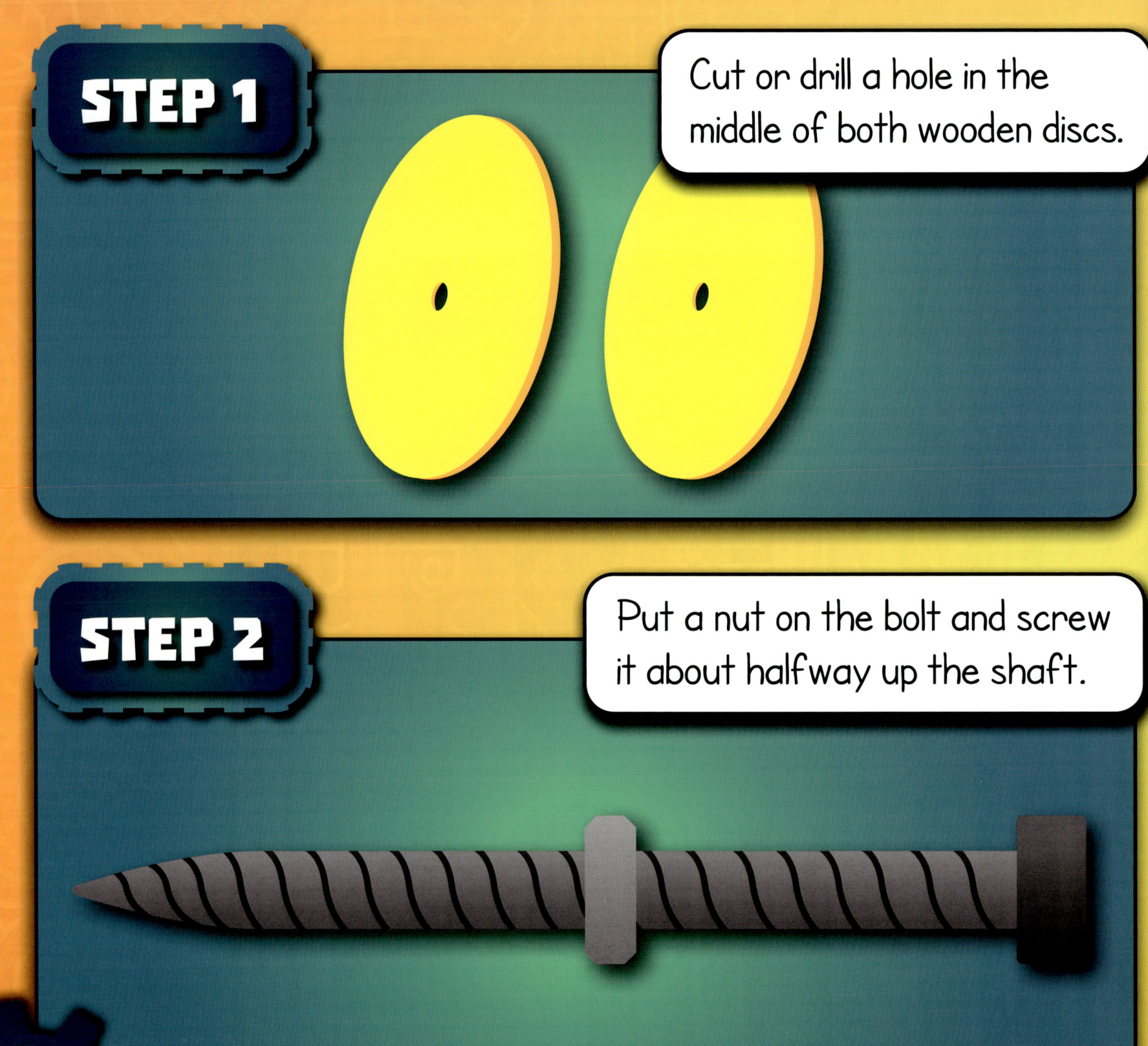

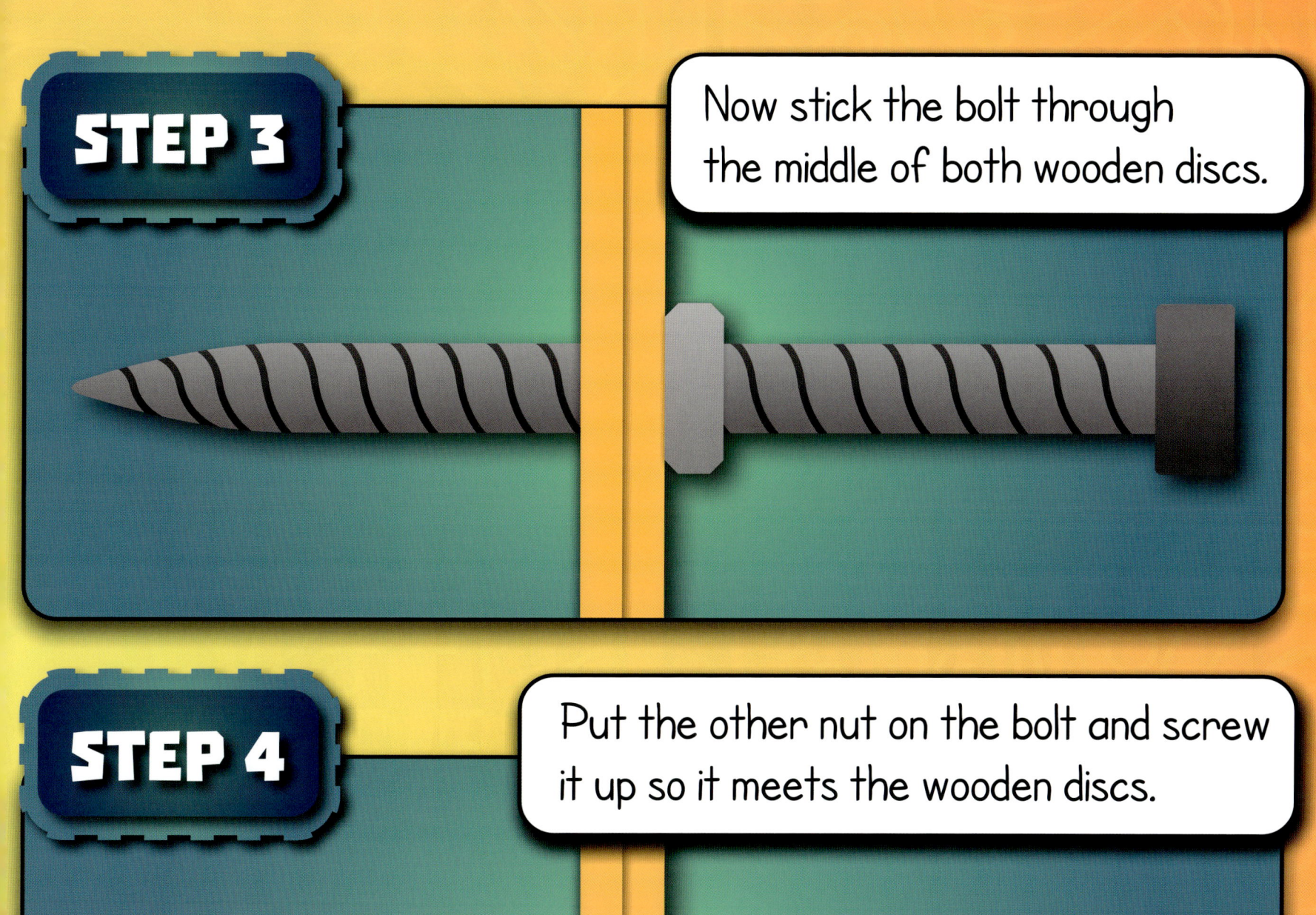

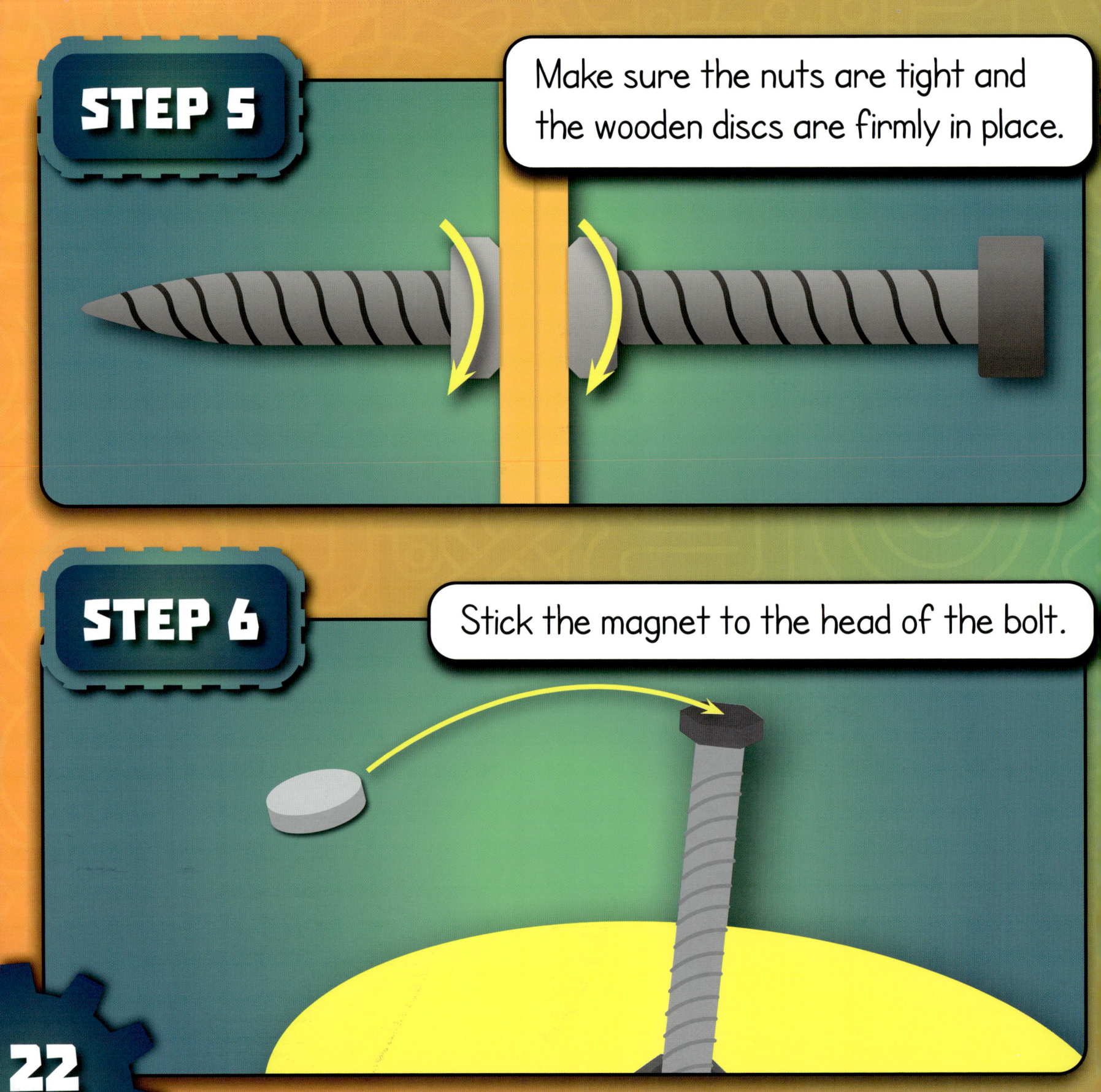

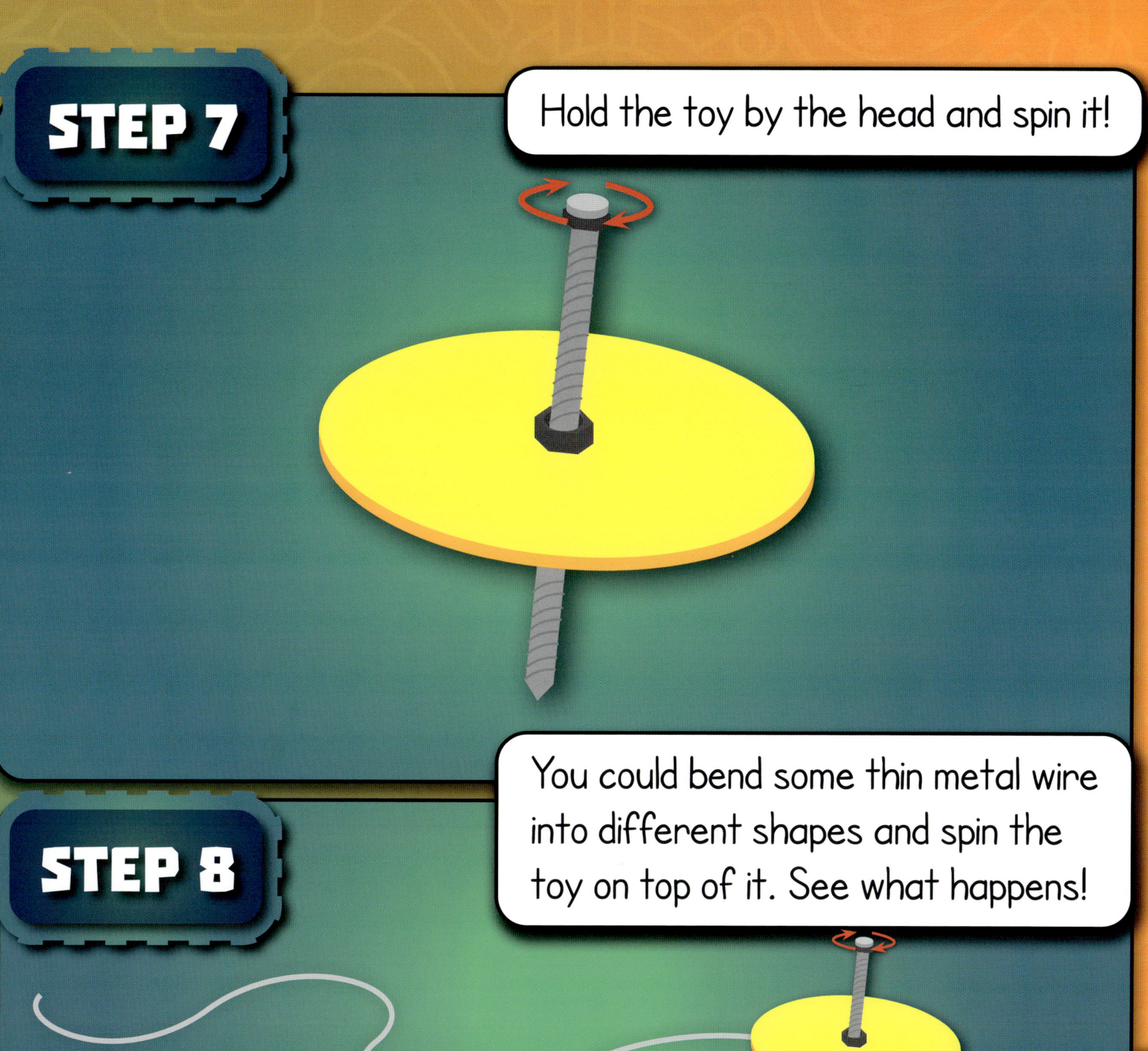

GLOSSARY

force	a push or pull on an object
friction	a force that slows things down and creates heat when two things rub together
material	a thing from which objects are made
motion	movement
ridge	a raised part that is long and thin, like a line
secure	safe and strong
universe	the space that everything exists in, including planets, galaxies and stars

INDEX

bolts 13, 15, 18–22
drills 7, 11, 18, 20
force 7, 14, 17
heads 10–12, 19, 22–23
metal 11, 13, 19, 23
nails 6–7
nuts 13, 19–22
plastic 8, 14
screwdrivers 7, 11–12
threads 10, 15–17